I0821406

Oceans
Maria Koran
EYEDISCOVER

Go to **www.eyediscover.com** and enter this book's unique code.

BOOK CODE

AVE35794

EYEDISCOVER brings you optic readalongs that support active learning.

Published by AV² by Weigl
350 5th Avenue, 59th Floor New York, NY 10118
Website: www.eyediscover.com

Library of Congress Control Number: 2019946280

ISBN 978-1-7911-0754-3 (hardcover)

Printed in Guangzhou, China
1 2 3 4 5 6 7 8 9 0 23 22 21 20 19

072019
121818

Project Coordinator: John Willis
Designers: Mandy Christiansen and Ana María Vidal

Weigl acknowledges Getty Images and iStock as the primary image suppliers for this title.

EYEDISCOVER provides enriched content, optimized for tablet use, that supplements and complements this book. EYEDISCOVER books strive to create inspired learning and engage young minds in a total learning experience.

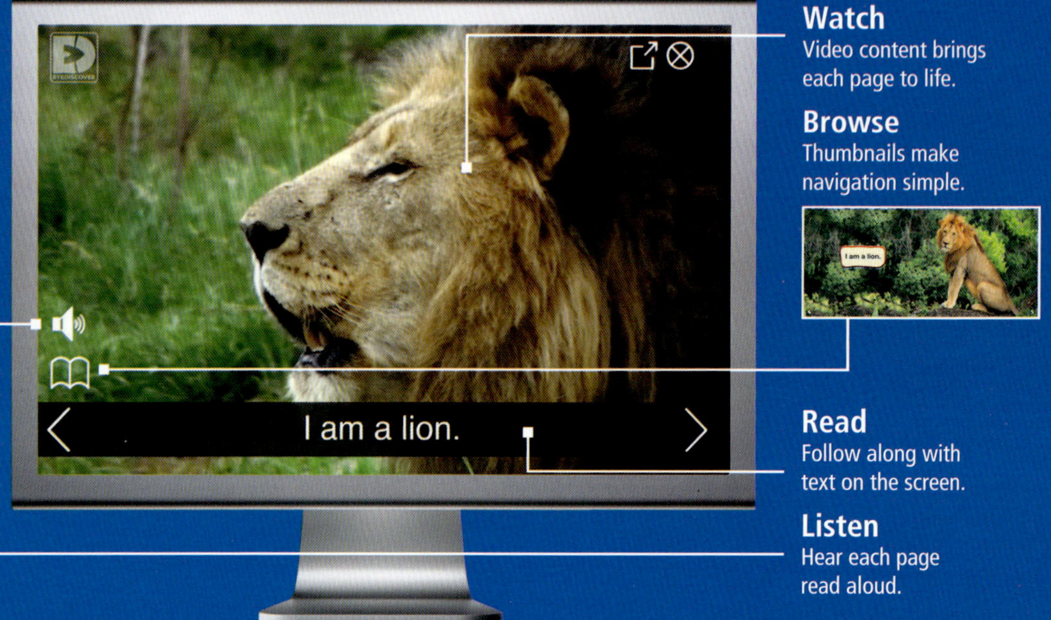

Watch
Video content brings each page to life.

Browse
Thumbnails make navigation simple.

Read
Follow along with text on the screen.

Listen
Hear each page read aloud.

Your EYEDISCOVER Optic Readalongs come alive with...

Audio
Listen to the entire book read aloud.

Video
High resolution videos turn each spread into an optic readalong.

OPTIMIZED FOR

- TABLETS
- WHITEBOARDS
- COMPUTERS
- AND MUCH MORE!

In this book, you will learn about

- what they are
- where they are
- what lives there

and much more!

Oceans cover most of Earth. Much of the air we breathe is made in the oceans.

6

There are five oceans. They are all connected. The Pacific Ocean is the largest ocean.

The largest animal in the ocean is the blue whale. The oceans are also home to tiny jellyfish.

Humpback whales travel each year. They spend summers in one ocean and have young in another.

Coral reefs are part of the oceans. The Great Barrier Reef is the largest coral reef in the world.

Oceans change the weather. They can cause large storms.

People use oceans to ship goods all over the world.

Many ocean animals and plants are in danger. Garbage affects life in the oceans.

The ocean is important to all life. People can help the ocean by keeping beaches clean.

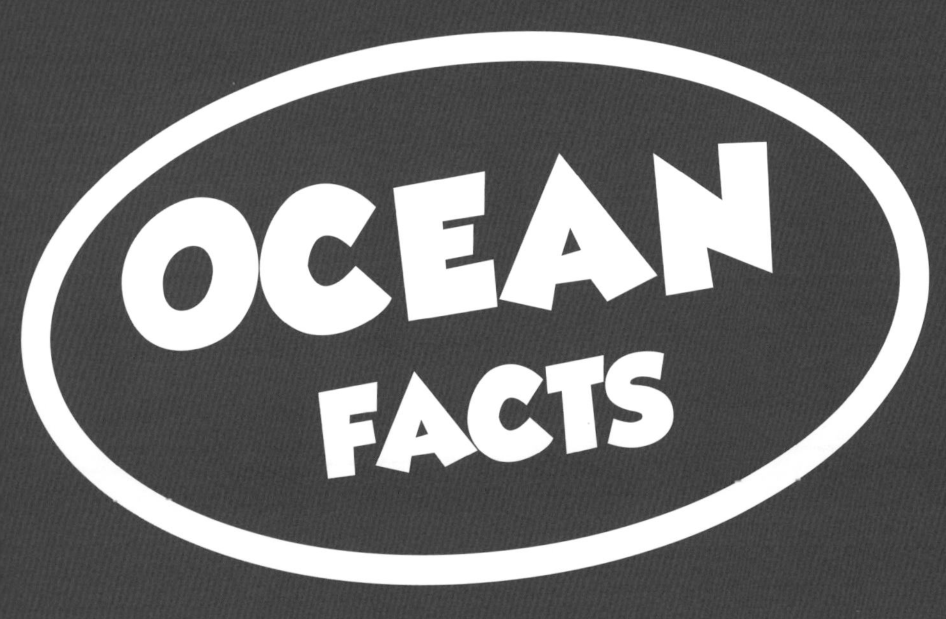

More than 70 percent of our planet's oxygen is produced by the oceans.

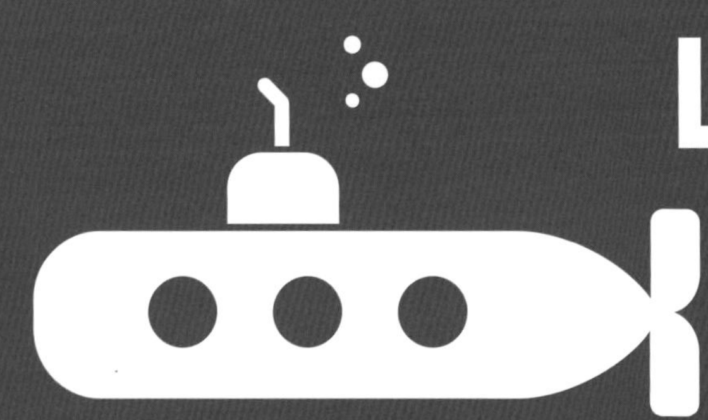

Less than 5 percent of the planet's oceans have been explored.

About 1 million different kinds of animals live in the ocean.

The Pacific Ocean contains more than 25,000 islands.

Coral produces its own sunscreen.

KEY WORDS

Research has shown that as much as 65 percent of all written material published in English is made up of 300 words. These 300 words cannot be taught using pictures or learned by sounding them out. They must be recognized by sight. This book contains 42 common sight words to help young readers improve their reading fluency and comprehension. This book also teaches young readers several important content words, such as proper nouns. These words are paired with pictures to aid in learning and improve understanding.

Page	Sight Words First Appearance
4	air, Earth, in, is, made, most, much, of, the, we
7	all, are, there, they
8	also, animal, home, it, to
11	and, another, each, have, one, year, young
12	great, part, world
15	can, change, large
16	goods, over, people, use
18	life, many, plants
21	by, help, important

Page	Content Words First Appearance
4	oceans
7	Pacific Ocean
8	blue whale, jellyfish
11	humpback whales, summers
12	coral reefs, Great Barrier Reef
15	storms, weather, winds
18	garbage
21	beaches

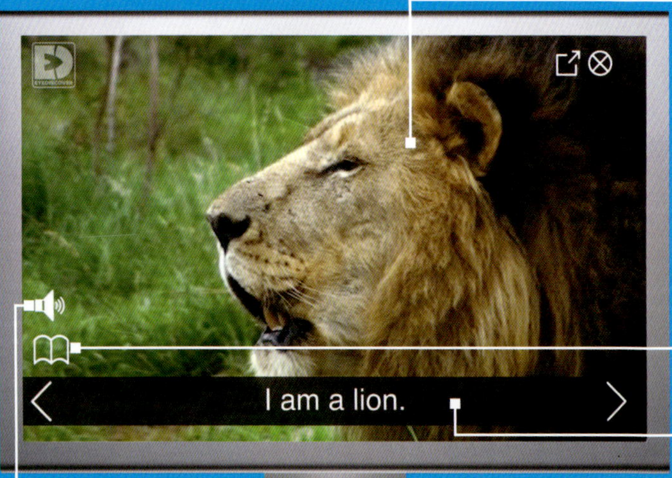

Watch
Video content brings each page to life.

Browse
Thumbnails make navigation simple.

Read
Follow along with text on the screen.

Listen
Hear each page read aloud.

Go to www.eyediscover.com and enter this book's unique code.

BOOK CODE

AVE35794